Songs of the Chippewa

SONGS OF THE CHIPPEWA

Adapted from the collections of Frances Densmore and

Henry Rowe Schoolcraft, and arranged for piano and guitar,

by JOHN BIERHORST/Pictures by JOE SERVELLO

FARRAR, STRAUS AND GIROUX   NEW YORK

Contents

The songs in this book were collected near the western shores of the Great Lakes by the ethnomusicologist Frances Densmore during the early 1900's and by the pioneer ethnographer Henry Rowe Schoolcraft more than half a century earlier. Students of Indian literature have long admired the clarity, the brevity, the haiku-like precision of the lyrics in Densmore's collections. The words to at least two of the Schoolcraft songs are well known in the literary adaptations of Longfellow:

> Ewa-yea! my little owlet!
> Who is this, that lights the wigwam?
> With his great eyes lights the wigwam?
> Ewa-yea! my little owlet!
>
> Wah-wah-taysee, little fire-fly,
> Little, flitting, white-fire insect,
> Little, dancing, white-fire creature,
> Light me with your little candle,
> Ere upon my bed I lay me,
> Ere in sleep I close my eyelids.
>
> *The Song of Hiawatha,*
> III, lines 81–4, 111–16

But Chippewa melodies, as opposed to lyrics, are comparatively little known, though they are of equal if not greater interest. It is the aim of the present collection to offer a representative sampling of this musical lore, with emphasis on fidelity to the recorded texts. In most cases the melodic lines are exactly as set down by Densmore, and in a few of the songs the original Chippewa words have been retained. In others, where Densmore's English translations are substituted, it has usually been necessary to re-word the lyric in order to preserve the musical line. In the case of the Schoolcraft songs, the music was never recorded. These lost melodies have here been replaced with melodies from Densmore, selected on the basis of mood, rhythm, and general artistic merit. The accompaniments have been kept as simple as possible, not only to make them accessible to beginning instrumentalists, but to keep them from over-whelming the songs themselves.

J. B.

Lullaby

repeat indefinitely

11

Song of the Deer Dancing

tee-bee-wenda-bah-no-gwen / whence does he spring?

eye-ya-bay / the deer

Beautiful Is Our Lodge

Beau - ti - ful as a star ____ hang - ing in the sky ___

____ is our lodge. ___ Here in com - pa - ny

with ___ the spir - it to - geth - - er we a - bide.

Sleep, Little Daughter

The Loons Are Singing

Hush, do you hear? Hear the loons sing-ing up in the sky.

Can you see o-ver the wood pass-ing by in the sky, fly-ing high sing-ing all

through the sky? Can you hear? Hear the loons sing-ing in the sky. _____

Light My Way to Bed

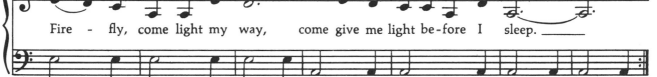

Come with your shin - ing white fire, come with your shin - ing white light.

Fire - fly, come light my way, come give me light be-fore I sleep. _____

Song to Make a Baby Laugh

A plump lit - tle pig hangs o - ver your bed. Four fun - ny feet it has, and a

lit - tle plump head. Here, no there, no here. Look a - way. _____

Flute Song

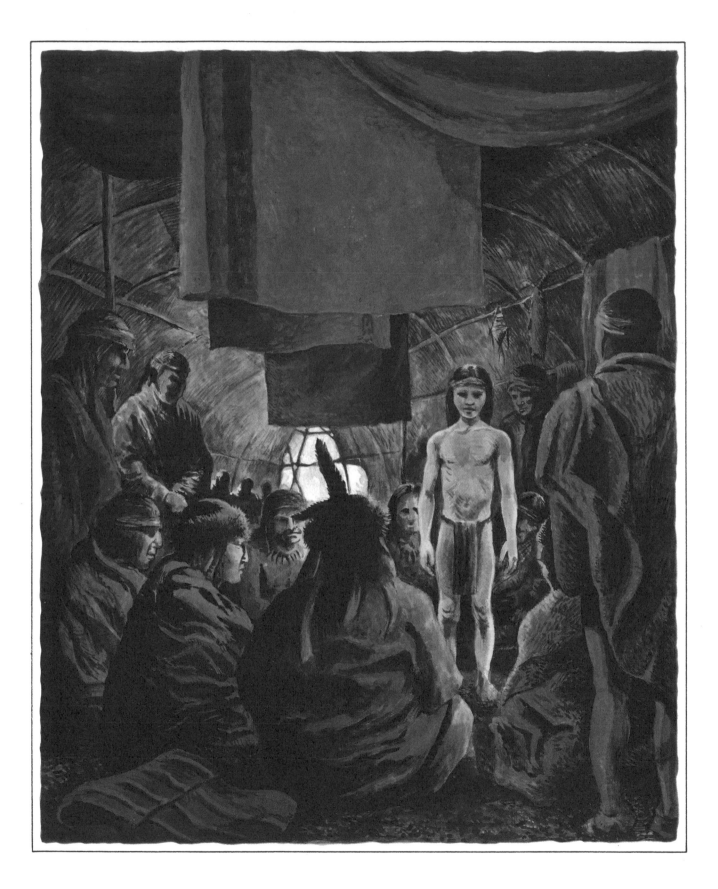

What Is This I Promise You?

What __ is this I pro - mise you?

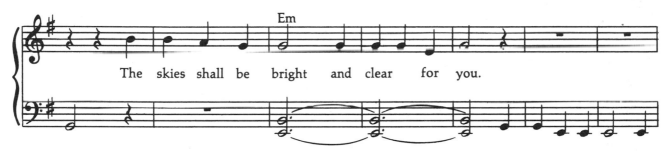

The skies shall be bright and clear for you.

This __ is what I pro - mise you. ____

Song of the Frog Waiting for Spring

1. Spir - its! you press me un - der! Spir - its! you
2. Why do you press me un - der? Why do you

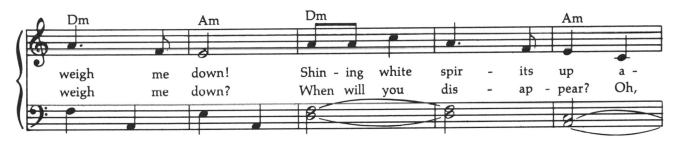

weigh me down! Shin - ing white spir - its up a -
weigh me down? When will you dis - ap - pear? Oh,

bove,____ why are you fall - ing down?____
when will you leave and spring re - turn?____

It Is I, the Little Owl

Very Much Afraid

eh-nee-wek   kah-yea   neen   eh - nee - wek   kah - yea   neen

ko - ko - ko   neen - go - sah _____   nay - jee - kay - wuh - bee - ah -

neen _____ ah bay ah ya,   bay ah   ya,   bay ah   ya,   bay ah   ya

eh-nee-wek / very much

kah-yea / also

neen / I

ko-ko-ko / of the owl

neen-go-sah / am afraid

nay-jee-kay-wuh-bee-ah-neen / when I'm sitting alone in the wigwam

ah bay ah ya / *nonsense syllables*

Dream Song

High in the sky I go, walk-ing in the sky I go, high a-bove the

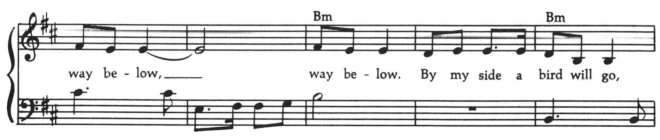

way be-low, _____ way be-low. By my side a bird will go,

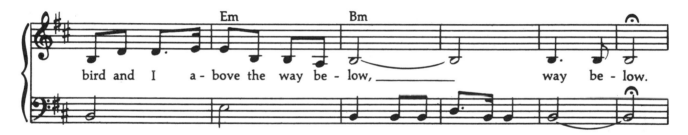

bird and I a-bove the way be-low, _____ way be-low.

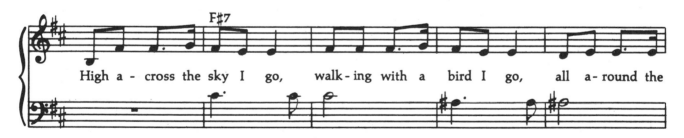

High a-cross the sky I go, walk-ing with a bird I go, all a-round the

sky we go, _____ all a-round we go, in the sky we go, bird and I. _____

Menominee Lullaby

Swing high - a - low gen - tly down, ___ up a - way a - gain

back and a - round, a - round and a - round not a

sound, hush- a - bye ba - by go gen - tly down. _____

repeat indefinitely

Song of a Boy Growing Up

ah- nee - nen-way- way   ah- nee - nen-way-way   wah- zee-swun im-bee - zin-

dah - go - nay

ah-nee-nen-way-way / the receding sound

wah-zee-swun / of the nest

im-bee-zin-dah-go-nay / I listen to it

The Spirit Will Appear

When the wa - ters are calm and the fog ris - es,

I the spir - it will now and then ap - pear.

Do Not Cry

kah-ee-gwoo / now

nee-mah-jah / I go

kay-go-soo / do not

mah-wee-ken / cry

Notes

The following abbreviations have been used to identify sources:

Schoolcraft 1845   Henry Rowe Schoolcraft, "Nursery and Cradle Songs of the Forest," *Oneota, or Characteristics of the Red Race in America*, 1845, pp. 212–20.

Schoolcraft 1853   _____, *Information Respecting the History, Condition and Prospects of the Indian Tribes of the United States*, Vol. III, 1853.

Schoolcraft 1855   Ibid., Vol. V, 1855.

Densmore 1910   Frances Densmore, *Chippewa Music*, Bureau of American Ethnology, Bulletin 45, 1910.

Densmore 1913   _____, *Chippewa Music–II*, Bureau of American Ethnology, Bulletin 53, 1913.

Densmore 1932   _____, *Menominee Music*, Bureau of American Ethnology, Bulletin 102, 1932.

PAGE 11 / *Lullaby*. The repeated *way way*, like the familiar English *rock-a-bye*, is used to suggest a gentle swinging motion. Words and music: Densmore 1913, no. 127.

PAGE 13 / *Song of the Deer Dancing*. Pronounce the words as though they were English. *Eye* rhymes with "my," etc. Words and music: Densmore 1913, no. 97.

PAGE 15 / *Beautiful Is Our Lodge*. A sacred song used in ceremonies of the Midewiwin, the Chippewa medicine society. Words and music adapted from Densmore 1910, no. 44.

PAGE 17 / *Sleep, Little Daughter*. Music adapted from Densmore 1932, no. 139. Words adapted from Schoolcraft 1845, p. 214. Schoolcraft adds the following description: "If the lodge be roomy and high, as lodges sometimes are, the cradle is suspended to the top poles to be swung. If not, or the weather be fine, it is tied to the limb of a tree, with small cords made from the inner bark of the linden, and a vibratory motion given to it from head to foot by the mother or some attendant. The motion thus communicated is that of a pendulum or common swing, and may be supposed to be the easiest and most agreeable possible to the child. It is from this motion that the leading idea of the cradle song is taken."

PAGE 19 / *The Loons Are Singing*. Most Indian songs are very brief. Like imagist poems or Japanese haiku, they merely symbolize an idea, an emotion, or an experience. As if to make up for the brevity, the singer repeats his song over and over again in a continuous chant— usually for the purpose of bringing about, as if by magic, something he desires very much. The loons, in this case, are an omen of victory in war. Words and music: Densmore 1910, no. 128 (the melody is unchanged; the words have been adapted).

PAGE 21 / *Light My Way to Bed*. For Longfellow's literary version, see p. 5 of this book. The Chippewa word for firefly is *wah-wah-taysee*. Words adapted from Schoolcraft 1855, p. 564. Music: Densmore 1910, no. 152.

PAGE 23 / *Song to Make a Baby Laugh*. Improvised hand motions and facial gestures make a simple game out of this little chant. Words and music adapted from Densmore 1913, no. 179.

PAGE 25 / *Flute Song*. Usually played on the pibegwun (Chippewa flute), but also hummed or crooned, especially by young men serenading their sweethearts. Densmore 1913, p. 42.

PAGE 27 / *What Is This I Promise You?* A sacred song, promising happiness and long life to the young Chippewa who devotes himself to the religion of his ancestors. Words and music adapted from Densmore 1910, no. 64.

PAGE 29 / *Song of the Frog Waiting for Spring*. Words adapted from Schoolcraft 1853, p. 329. Music adapted from Densmore 1913, no. 37.

PAGE 31 / *It Is I, the Little Owl*. For Longfellow's engaging but distorted version, see p. 5 of this book. Words adapted from Schoolcraft 1845, pp. 213–14. Music freely adapted from Densmore 1913, no. 39.

PAGE 33 / *Very Much Afraid.* All Chippewa children were taught to fear the owl. This chant is said to have been composed by a little boy one night when his mother had gone to visit a neighbor. Alone in the wigwam, he became frightened of the owl and began to sing. People in nearby wigwams overheard him, picked up the song, and eventually it became known throughout the village. *Eh* rhymes with "say," *nee* with "see," *wek* with "neck," etc. Words and music: Densmore 1910, no. 121.

PAGE 35 / *Dream Song.* Words and music adapted from Densmore 1913, no. 85.

PAGE 37 / *Menominee Lullaby.* A melody used by the Menominee of Wisconsin, a tribe closely related to the Chippewa, who now live mostly in Minnesota. The words are my own, based on suggestions given in Schoolcraft 1845, pp. 212–15. Music: Densmore 1932, no. 140.

PAGE 39 / *Song of a Boy Growing Up.* American Indian songs are admired by musicians the world over for their intricate rhythms. This rather difficult chant, requiring some practice before it can be sung, is a good example. Words and music: Densmore 1913, no. 100. Densmore adds that the song is associated with the old Indian custom requiring youths to hold fasting vigils in the wilderness. Her informant learned it as a boy from his grandfather. When the grandson had blackened his face and was ready to go forth alone from the camp, he danced while the old man sang.

PAGE 41 / *The Spirit Will Appear.* Another sacred song used in Midewiwin ceremonies. Words and music adapted from Densmore 1910, no. 27.

PAGE 43 / *Do Not Cry.* The mournful, haunting melody identifies this as a typical Indian love song. Words and music: Densmore 1913, no. 106.

Music autographing by Maxwell Weaner
Designed by Jane Byers Bierhorst
Printed by Reehl Litho, Inc., New York City
Bound by A. Horowitz and Son, Clifton, New Jersey